Xmas 1978
from Mom

Betsy Joyce

FLORENCE

Text by
Pierre Leprohon

Translated by David Macrae

Minerva

FLORENCE

CONTENTS

Credits : Arboit : End-papers - 3 - 7 - 9 - 20 - 21 - 23 - 24b, c - 25 -
27 - 35 - 37 - 40 - 41b - 42b - 43 - 46a - 46c - 50 - 51 - 56 - 57 -
58 - 59 - 60b - 61 - 64 - 65 - 80 - 82 - 86b - 91 - 94a - 98 - 100 -
Chauvaud/Fotogram : 109 - D.R. : 63 - 70 - Dulevant : 19 - 48 -
49 - Fiore : 30a, b - 75 - Gemini : 46b - 76 - 79b - Leprohon : 4 -
22 - 24a - 34 - 38 - 41a - 60a - 84 - 85 - 87 - 94b - 95b - 96 - 100 -
104 - 106 - Pizzi : 5 - 10 - 16 - 26a - 66 - 68 - 74 - 79a - 81b - 99 -
101 - 103a - 105 - S.E.F. : 18b - 47 - Simion/Ricciarini : 88 - 89 -
Tomsich/Ricciarini : 8 - 12 - 44 - 71 - 78 - 93 - Tourenne/Fotogram :
18a - 33 - Unedi : 5 - 28 - 30 - 39 - 54 - 67 - 69 - 72 - 73 - 90 - 92 -
112.

ISBN 0.517.241129

© Editions Minerva, S.A., Genève, 1978.
Printed in Italy

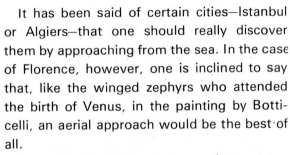

FLORENCE

It has been said of certain cities—Istanbul or Algiers—that one should really discover them by approaching from the sea. In the case of Florence, however, one is inclined to say that, like the winged zephyrs who attended the birth of Venus, in the painting by Botticelli, an aerial approach would be the best of all.

The ideal starting point for a visitor arriving in this way would be the Piazzale Michelangelo, which looks out over the left bank of the river, or, better still, the San Miniato terrace, which stands on the side of a hill. From both these vantage points the city spreads out like an open flower—some would say like a slightly faded bouquet in the bluish vase of the Val d'Arno. One has no sensation of being enclosed by the valley, the sides of which rise evenly and gracefully towards the sky. Down below, a harmonious panorama of rust-red rooftops and bright façades, with occasional domes and bell-towers. Indeed the entire city seems to have come straight out of the past, with none of its modern activities, streets, bustle and crowds. At a single glance, one can encompass several centuries, while the modern age seems to have stepped modestly aside... Seen from the slopes of the Oltrarno, Florence has lost none of its integrity. The gently sloping hills beyond the city are dotted here and there with villas and bell-towers.

Yet Florence is certainly not a dead town,

any more than Venice is. Nor is it a living museum. It seems to have emerged from the past virtually unscathed, and to have brought that past with it, for us to see. The joy that one feels on visiting cities such as Pompei or Carthage derives merely from the sight of ruins and dust. But here, the city's lifeblood is still flowing, among the monuments built by so many past generations, while the most fragile works of art—frescoes and paintings—greet the modern visitor with a veritable symphony of lovely colours.

Florence has been shaped by history and art. Looking out over it from the terrace of San Miniato, one is struck by its extraordinary balance and harmony. There is something musical about its perfect unity: a marvellous polyphonic chorus of diverses styles, from medieval to Renaissance, in which genius and greatness, nobility and glory, are evenly matched.

Yet, as our imaginary visitor moves down from the pedestal of the Piazzale Michelangelo, where he has begun his stay in Florence, he realizes that this first impression is unreliable, that the city is, after all, secret and that its apparent unity is really contrast... Even before he has crossed the river, at the foot of the ramparts, he finds himself in a purely medieval scene, hemmed in by narrow streets and austere buildings. Some distance further on, however, the palaces erected by great princely families present to the world

a rather forbidding immensity of scale, with their windows covered by grillwork and their haughty façades—all in all, not what one would call a human scale of dimensions... The miraculous thing about Florence is that, despite its monumental aspect, it still appeals directly to the heart. Could its charm have something to do, perhaps, with the wonderful gardens which lie beyond the closed palaces, and the sunlit squares which one enters after passing along shaded side-streets?

This contrast is to be found not only in the things of the present, but also in the memories left by the past. This city of art was also the scene of some fierce and bloody conflicts. All one has to do is to disturb the dust of the centuries in order to glimpse the violent interplay of ambitions, plots and crimes...

What an amazing place! Those who built this city and those who sullied its name, those who added to its beauty and those who betrayed it, all now lie dead in their marble tombs: their very deaths have become creative themes. Everything has been erased, save the beauty of their testimony, which, though left behind to perpetuate their own glory, now adds to our pleasure and enchantment. It is to this beauty that we shall now turn.

A glimpse of the Piazza della Signoria.

6

I. A CITY NAMED AFTER FLOWERS

"Florida Florentia".

The Romans founded the city which now bears the name Firenze. The Etruscans, who were the masters of this region from the 5th to the 2nd century BC, had settled some distance away, on a hill six kilometers from the Arno, where they founded Fiesole. Earlier still, between the 10th and the 8th centuries BC, the Italics, an Indo-European people from the north, had occupied the region though thay later faded away as the Etruscan dominion became established.

Sensing the value of the passage towards the Po, Caesar, in 59 BC, ordered the creation of a colony on the northern bank of the river. The settlement is thought to have been founded in spring, during the floral games, or "Ludi Florales"; this would account for the city's name, Florentia. Flora was the goddess of flowers and gardens, and the mother of spring, in Roman mythology. From the Latin *Florentia*, the Tuscans derived *Fiorenzia* — a term which may be read on various Renaissance frescoes, and which later became contracted to *Firenze.*

There are virtually no remains of the original city left in Florence. It had been situated on the site of the present Piazza della Repubblica, with a forum and four gates, accessible from two streets which crossed at right angles in the central square. The route to the river lay beyond the southern gate.

At the end of the 2nd century, about

Panoramic view from the top of the cathedral: left, the church of Santa Croce; in the middle, the Bargello; in the background, the hills, with their villas, gardens and sanctuaries. Below, old houses near the cathedral.

Facing, entrance to an Etruscan tomb near the city. Right, a view of Florence in times gone by.

10,000 people lived here. The city had expanded past its original walls, with the construction of a theater, thermal baths and an aqueduct. About this time, Syrian merchants, doubtless from the port of Pisa, settled in Florence and introduced Christiannity. The Palestinian saint Felicity was honored there. Minias, one of the members of this eastern Christian settlement, was maryrized in 250, under the reign of Decius, and was buried on the hill where the church of San Miniato—named after him—now stands. One of the first bishops of the city, Zenobius, was also of eastern origins, like another Palestinian saint, Reparata.

This infiltration from the Orient could quite possibly have influenced the formation of the Florentine character, particularly as it helped spread the Christian faith on the ruins of paganism.

Then came the invasions from the north, which Byzantium proved unable to repel: the Huns of Attila, mentioned by Dante, the Ostrogoths of Totila, and lastly the Lombards.

It was not until the arrival ot the Carolingians that Florence emerged from the languor of several centuries. In 854 Lothair I merged the counties of Florence and Fiesole, thus sealing the decline of the ancient Etruscan settlement at the expense of its neighbor in the valley. Soon, the rise in the volume of trade passing through the city of the flowers began to augur well for its future.

The Hungarian threat in the 10th century did nothing to slow down its burgeoning growth. The construction, early in the 11th century, of the monastery and church of San Miniato (1014-1050) made it clear that the masters of Florence intended the city's destiny to be a glorious one. Its prestige was confirmed in 1055, with the holding of the council, presided over by the Pope, in the presence of Emperor Henry III and 120 bishops. Two years later, Gherardo, bishop of Florence, became pope, under the name Nicholas III, but he remained faithful to his city, where he died in 1061. A Florentine knight, Giovanni Gualberto, founder of the Carthusian monastery of Vallombrosa, showed the way to the restoration of the Christian virtues which had been sadly neglected by the clerics of his age. Florence was to become an important spiritual center.

The conflicts of the Middle Ages.

Having saved Europe from the Hungarian peril and triumphed over the princes, Emperor Otto had himself proclaimed king of Pavia, and then went to Rome to see the pope, his intention being to restore the empire of Charlemagne. On February 2, 962, he was crowned Emperor of the West by Pope John XII. This title, however, soon gave rise to a clash of authority, both spiritual and

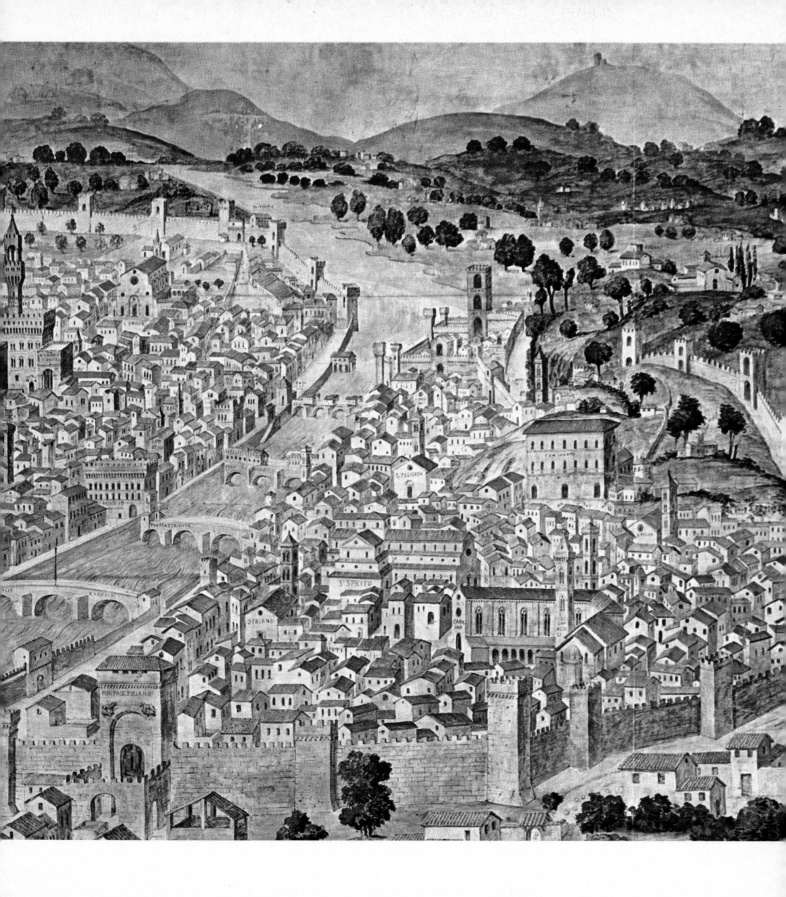

temporal, which was to overshadow the whole of European history for three centuries.

In Germany, one Emperor Otto succeeded another. A century after the death of Otto I, the quarrel over lay investiture sharply aggravated the conflict between Emperor Henry IV and Pope Gregory VII. Florence was then under the control of Countess Mathilda, countess of Tuscany, wife of the king of Bavaria and an ally of the pope. In July 1082, after a siege lasting ten days, the emperor had to withdraw his forces; this was a victory for the people of Florence, and one which strengthened its firm conviction as to the role the city could and should play.

After the death of Countess Mathilda this popular determination was directed towards the commune itself, and against the princely heirs and the noble families—particularly the Alberti—who had planned to move in to take the place of the imperial authority.

About the same time, through the interplay of alliances, there was an increase in rivalry between the Italian cities. Florence found the proximity of Fiesole disturbing, as it might serve as a bridgehead for attacks by enemies, so it found a pretext, in 1125, for destroying the smaller city. All that remained intact was the dome and the bishops's residence; the territory of Fiesole was henceforth part of Florence. This was the first act whereby the city was to show its grand ambitions, and it occurred just when it had for the first time acquired sufficient inner cohesion and strength to impose its will on others.

A commune comes of age.

The imperial legate had, in fact, recognized the authority of the commune of Florence since the middle of the 12th century; but its independence was not approved until 1183,

after the signing of the general peace between Pope Lucius III and Frederick Barbarossa. The city was then controlled by a college of consuls who could be re-appointed every two months and who were chosen from among the nobility and the ordinary people, or, more exactly, the bourgeoisie. The prerogatives of the clergy were gradually whittled away, to the advantage of two other classes of citizens: the *milites,* or mounted soldiers entrusted with the defense of the city, and the merchants.

The life of the commune already depended heavily on trade, perhaps particularly so at the end of the 12th century. This was the origin of its later wealth, power and renown. Because of its geographical function as a kind of turntable in a rapidly changing Europe, Florence was in contact, through Genoa and Pisa, with the western world and through Venice with the Middle East, while it also had contacts with the Germanic countries to the north and the pontifical regions to the south. Hence the need to assure the security of trade routes and the support of the maritime cities. This dual purpose involved Florence in struggles with the feudal lords who carried out raids and exacted tolls on its territories, and led to its alliance with Pisa against Genoa, in an effort to find and outlet for its western traffic.

Florence was already a city of more than 25,000 inhabitants. It had already spilled over the left bank of the Arno and built a fifth enclosure covering about 120 acres. Contemporaries dubbed it "flourishing Florence", *Florida florentia.* It took barely two more centuries to reach its apex, though in the process it had to endure endless conflicts, not just with foreign powers, but also within its own walls.

Guelphs and Ghibellines.

An early crisis occurred in 1193 over the choice of consuls, which had previously been the exclusive domain of a few influential families. The outcome was the introduction of the régime of the *podestat,* a magistrate from outside the commune, and thus presumably impartial in his judgments; this system was common to a number of cities in Tuscany and Umbria. Nonetheless, the crisis marked the beginning of the rivalries which, over a span of three centuries, were to divide the *popolo grasso,* finally eliminate the nobility, and, by means of alliances, draw the commune into the centuries-long duel between the empire and the papacy.

Originally, two Germanic families aspired to the imperial crown: that of the Hohenstaufen, after which one of Barbarossa's castles, Weiblingen, was named, and that of the Welfs, who enjoyed the support of Otto of Brunswick and the papacy; the two names were Latinized, respectively, as Ghibellines and Guelphs.

Without giving a detailed account of the varying fortunes of the two sides in these struggles of the 13th and 14th centuries, during which control of the city alternated between one or other of the factions, we shall mention certain noteworthy aspects of the period. First, the fact that the commune never lost its independence, despite a multitude of difficulties. In 1268 Charles of Anjou, who was supported by the pope against the empire, entered Florence; yet he was unable to remain there, even though he enjoyed the favor of the Guelphs. In 1342, Gautier de Brenne, Duke of Athens, was named "lord for life". This lasted for eight months, after which the bourgeoisie resumed control.

Early in the 15th century a split occurred among the Guelphs, dividing the Florentines, this time, into Blacks and Whites!

The Whites were driven out of town—with Dante amongst them—but the Blacks also suffered some reversals of fortune. Florence had to endure further disasters: the bankruptcy of the Bardi in 1346 took the entire city to the brink of calamity. Next year, the Black Death felled a good half of the population. Yet Florence again recovered.

Another characteristic trait: the perennial nature of the oligarchic régime, in which power passed through a succession of hands, but always for the benefit of the *popolo grasso,* whose policy of economic expansion gave the city its wealth and eminence.

The oligarchic regime.

The major families of Florence, having created the city's prosperity, were quite determined to be in charge of its destiny. All activity was organized in the *arti,* or guilds, but only the *Arti majores,* and particularly the *Arte di Calamala,* which comprised the entire cloth trade, had control over the government. The medium and the minor guilds —oil and wine merchants, innkeepers, small craftsmen, bakers, etc., and, of course, the *popolo minuto* (workers and employees)— had no say at all in the conduct of the city's affairs! Several attempts were made to change the oligarchy to a democracy, but they came to nothing.

The political privileges enjoyed by the *popolo grasso* at least had the advantage of tending, first of all, towards the advancement of the city as a whole. The wealth and glory of the principal families were also to the credit of the city. Knowing that business lay at the basis of this prosperity, the Florentine *aediles* concentrated on it above all else, leaving military questions, the defense of the city and even territorial conquest in the hands of the famous *Condottieri.* And even the conquests themselves—Pistoïa in 1228, Sienna in 1229, Pisa, conquered by Genoa in 1284 and annexed by Florence in 1406, Livorno acquired in 1421—were intended only as ways of eliminating competition or improving access to markets. Florence allowed the cities under its control the right to manage their own affairs.

This business-minded bourgeoisie,

Orsanmichele: a medallion ot the school of Della Robbia.

however, had more than economic expansion in mind: it built palaces and churches, and had the municipal buildings adorned with statues and frescoes. It clearly intended that Florence was to be both the richest and the most beautiful of cities. This determination of theirs served as a stimulus to the spirit of contemporary Florentines, and beginning with the genius of Dante and Giotto in the fourteenth century, led to a veritable outpouring of artistic talent. Merchants they certainly were, those men of the *popolo grasso,...* but they were also patrons of the arts. It is fitting to recall that Maecenas, the original model for patrons of the arts, at the beginning of the Christian era, was a natire of Arezzo, in other words a Tuscan.

After the Peruzzi, Bonaccorso and Bardi families, a new generation took command: the Alberti, Ricci, Strozzi and Medicis, all of whom pursued the same policies and had the same ambitions as their predecessors. While Rome fell into lethargy during the period of the Avignon papacy (1309-1377), Florence became one of the major intellectual, artistic and economic centers of Western Europe. It had expanded and consolidated its power. A ring of fortified battlements enclosed its residences and its palaces, all the way to the slopes of the Oltrarno. Sixty square towers stood at regular intervals along this wall. Even the rivalry of the rich and powerful contributed to the beauty of the city.

The Florence of the Medicis.

Giovanni de Medicis, who had been elected *gonfalonier* in 1421, inaugurated a policy which enabled his descendants, despite the vagaries of fortune, to remain masters of Florence for nearly three centuries. As defined by André Barret, this policy involved "playing with the power of the people without actually entrusting them with that power". Giovanni de Medicis had won the favor of the *popolo minuto.* His son, Cosimo—known as the Elder—succeeded even more completely in governing without displaying his power. He proved able to please the ordinary people by organising festivities, erecting buildings and keeping the city's business prosperous. His great generosity towards artists promoted, and perhaps even led to a great blossoming of genius in the arts and sciences.

His grandsons, Lorenzo and Giuliano, came to power in 1432. Rival families, however, had not disarmed. In 1478 the Pazzi Conspiracy cost the life of the second of the two brothers. Lorenzo tightened his grip on the city. The Republic was a mere façade, masking the power of a tyrant. Even so, Lorenzo the Magnificent certainly deserved his title. He was on easy terms with the ordinary people, and led a simple, happy life. He treated artists as his friends and Michelangelo as his son. He wielded his influence across Europe and reigned in lavish

16

This famous painting—the Adimari-Ricasoli wedding on the Piazza San Giovanni—brings alive the beauty, the extreme refinement and the charm of life in Florence during the Renaissance.

Below, one of the narrow medieval streets, many of which are still to be found in the city. Right, portrait of Julian de Medicis.

style. The papacy, however, found his ambitions increasingly disturbing: it accordingly instigated the Pazzi conspirators, and withdrew from him the administration of the pontifical finances. When Peter, Lorenzo's successor, opened the gates of the city to Charles VIII, king of France, it was the end of the popularity of the Medicis.

The monk Savonarola, who had lashed out at corruption and preached austerity, set up a new republic, stigmatising all human joy in the process. Four years later he was burned publicly. The "golden age" ended in blood and confusion!

The Medicis came back to power in 1512, only to be driven out, fifteen years later. Pope Clement VII—Giuliano's bastard son—appealed to Charles V to restore his family to power in Florence. It took a siege lasting eleven months before he did so. This victory marked the end of the agreement between the city and its rulers: the Medicis were to hang on for almost another two centuries, but now they ruled Tuscany as tyrants.

In 1734, through the interplay of treaties, the duchy passed to the house of Lorraine, and thence to the Austrian Empire. Now Florence was no more than the capital of a duchy over which the imperial forces and Napoleon were to wrangle. The 1848 uprising was a prelude to the *Risorgimento.* In 1860 a plebiscite decided in favor of the annexation of the duchy to the kingdom of Piedmont-

The print shown below depicts the assassination of Julian de Medicis during the Pazzi Conspiracy.
Right, inner courtyard of a Renaissance palace.

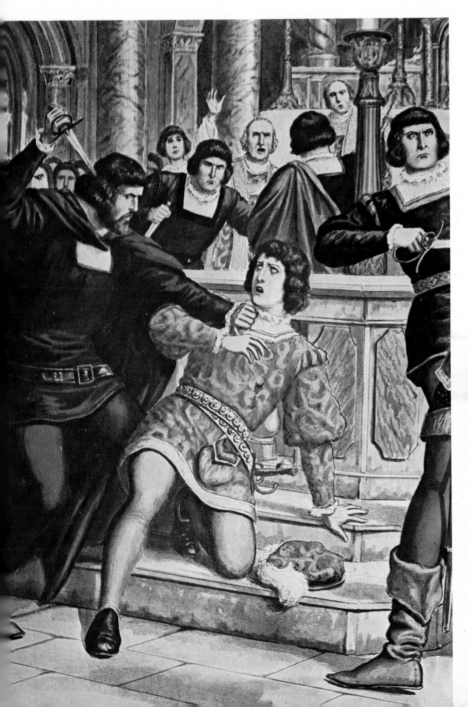

Sardinia, and then to Italy. For a few years—1865-1871—Florence was the capital of the new State; in that capacity it was the creation of the first institutions, the Parliament and the new ministries. With the influx of civil servants the population of Florence rose considerably. New roads were built and the palaces were modernized. Intellectual life flourished, to match the city's new political role, and the Florentine dialect served as the basis for the restoration of Italian.

After the fall of Rome in 1870, Florence lost its status of capital city, but it still remained the most brilliant focal point of artistic and intellectual life in the new Italy.

2. THE LIGHTHOUSES OF THE CITY

Seen from any of its numerous vantage points, Florence leaves imprinted on one's mind—and later on one's memory—the image òf its elegant domes and towers. First of all, the *campanile* and the dome of Santa Maria dei Fiori, and, facing them, the two towers of the Palazzo Vecchio and the Bargello. These monuments tower above the rooftops which they appear to protect; they are, in a sense, the lighthouses of Florence. They are a concise expression of its destiny during the few centuries in which it came to be so predominant, evoking its struggles and triumphs, and its dual nature, both religious and civic. Frequently, in these spendid monuments one catches a glimpse, too, of the passion and tragedy of Florentine history: the flagstones of Santa Maria bloodied by a political crime and a monk dying at the stake outside the walls of the Palazzo Vecchio!

These two structures also reflect the twin yet contradictory traits of the city's past: beauty and horror. In fact, the entire history of the city is written within the small space between the Duomo and the Palazzo. As we have seen, this was also the site of its birth.

From the battlements of the Palazzo Vecchio to the Brunelleschi dome, from the Bargello to the Baptistery, one finds all the

The two most famous towers of the city: the Campanile (by Giotto) and the tower of the Palazzo Vecchio.

styles represented, from Romanesque to Renaissance. All forms of artistic expression are found here, in abundance: mosaic, fresco, terra cotta, painting, sculpture, architecture... It would be difficult to find anywhere else such a profusion of sublimely beautiful things.

The visitor would do well to just walk from one to the other, seeking to form his own impressions before attempting a proper study, catching the smile of a stone cherub, noticing a particularly fine color, discovering a bas-relief or some exceptional piece of perspective... These two structures, which the passage of time has brought together, lie only a few hundred paces apart. Via Calzaioli, which, like the other thoroughfares of Florence, is lively and noisy, leads from the Piazza del Duomo to the Piazza della Signoria.

This, besides being the artistic center of Florence, is also the center of its mundane activities; there is nothing separating the historic city from the modern metropolis. Instead, the action of modern life takes place on a stage built centuries ago. Just as the various styles and periods are to be seen side by side in the architecture of Florence, so also on its streets foreign tourists and local people mingle naturally. The city of flowers does not want to be thought of as a museum-piece. The offices of the Republic are housed in palaces built by the Medicis, while the rites of Vatican II are celebrated on the altars of the city's churches.

Two views of the Cathedral of Santa-Maria-dei-Fiori.

Baptistery, Dome and *Campanile.*

In keeping with the Italian — and especially Tuscan— formula, the cathedral of Florence consists of three independent elements: the Baptistery, the Bell-tower and the Dome, which is the church itself. These elements are not from the same, period; rather, they have come in a succession since the 11th century, when the present city is deemed to have been founded. Everything prior to that had virtually disappeared, while the city's "golden age" is situated in the 14th and 15th centuries.

The Baptistery of Saint John, which was originally a cathedral, is the nucleus of the Christian city. Its origins, which are uncertain, are thought to lie somewhere between the 6th and the 11th centuries; its design, so similar to that of the Roman Pantheon, reveals some ancient influences. Its octagonal shape gives it a somewhat closed air, a secret majesty, further ennobled by the mosaics of the cupola. Its Romanesque arches, the balance of each architectural section, its geometrical decoration of white and green marble and its exquisite floors constitute a sort of prelude to Tuscan religious art. It was here that Dante was baptized.

Even more than the interior, it is the outside of the Baptistery which makes it such a truly splendid work of art: the harmony of its marble and particularly the gilded bronze

Assorted views of the façade of the cathedral.

External view of the Baptistery, opposite the cathedral. Below, a Renaissance procession between the two buildings. Right, one of the sculptures of the main entrance and inner view of the Baptistery.

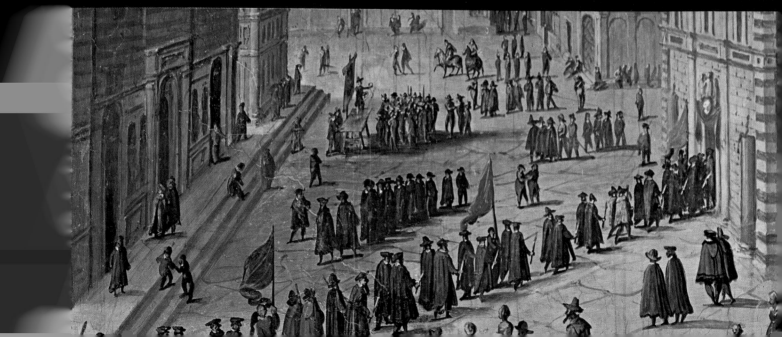

The choir of the Cathedral.

panels of its three doors. These were built between 1330 and 1452, the first by Andrea Pisano, and the others by Ghiberti after a competition in which he defeated Brunelleschi and Donatello, and which took 20 years of his life !

Michelangelo gave his name to the last of them, thus assuring that it was worthy of "paradise". Can it be said, however, that the panels of Pisano, which are more highly stylized, are inferior to the biblical scenes depicted with such immense graphic exuberance by Ghiberti? From one century to another, the art of the sculptors passed from the Middle Ages to the Renaissance, together with its prolific imagination and symbols.

A sort of square—for some years now fortunately free of cars—separates the baptistery from the dome. It can be reached by a few steps, on which one frequently sees foreign tourists sitting for a moment's rest. In contrast to the elegant simplicity of the baptistery of Saint John stands the façade of Saint Mary of the Flowers, which, having remained incomplete for many years was remodelled several times and finally decorated at the end of the 19th century with a profusion of motifs, niches and pediments which the visitor might find a bit overpowering!

Santa Maria dei Fiori... of course, what other name could have been given to the Virgin of Florence! Rejecting its eastern origins, the Christian commune had placed itself under the protection of Saint John; but it was to Mary that it dedicated the cathedral which was to replace that of Saint Reparata, and for which it turned to the best architect of the day, Arnolfo di Cambio. Construction began in 1296 and lasted one and a half centuries. After Cambio's death, Giotto took charge of operations, including work on the bell-tower, and it was Andrea Pisano and lastly Talenti (1349-1369) who gave the building its present size.

The cupola was designed and built by Brunelleschi. It is a masterpiece of daring and harmony which crowns the dome as a whole: "to everyone's alarm, the inspired calculator went ahead and placed on the top of the structure its heavy marble head, the lantern, scoffing at their fears."

As soon as the visitor passes through the main door—said to have been designed by Lorenzo the Magnificent—he is instantly struck by the sheer vastness of the nave. Santa Maria is the biggest church in Italy. It is also one of the most severe, its stark surfaces contrasting powerfully with the richness of its external decorative detail. A meeting place rather than a place of prayer... a closed place, full of history: Giuliano de Medicis dying under the dagger of the assassins, while Lorenzo flees from choir to sacristy... Savonarola terrorizing and overwhelming the crowds packed into this immense edifice. The immense frescoes of mounted *condottieri* which adorn its walls are also typical

Left, the cupola over the cathedral choir.
Facing, the Pieta by Michelangelo.
Below, detail of the Campanile.

of the austere character of Santa Maria dei Fiori, which does so little to live up to its own name! If Mary is present here at all, it is the Mary of sorrow who, with Magdalen and Nicodemus, holds up the dead body of Christ in the admirable Pieta in the transept, and which Michelangelo could not, as in so many other instances, complete...

As for the Campanile, which stands next to the dome without actually belonging to it, it can safely be described as the triumph of the irrational! It is certainly not a watch-tower, while the function of holding up church bells can hardly justify the lavish ornamentation which covers it from top to bottom, between its lattice windows.

In fact, the sole justification for the Campanile is its nobility and its beauty. It was to be built, in the words of a contemporary, so as to "exceed in height, magnificence and perfection whatever the Greeks and Romans might have done in the same genre." This task was entrusted to Giotto, who, having drawn up the plans in 1334, died two years later; as in the case of the Dome, Andrea Pisano and Francesco Talenti carried out the work of construction on the basis of Giotto's plans.

It is a geometric symphony of white Carrara marble, of green marble from Prato, pink marbles from Maremma, highlighted with sculptural variations: the bas-reliefs by Pisano are thought to have been based on designs by Giotto. Mythological scenes, allegories and symbols, work in the fields, the rhythm of the seasons... Statues by Donatello adorn the niches—a highly irrational place for them to be, so high above the ground as to be virtually indecipherable! Yet the men of the *trecento* knew that art was like life, in the sense that its mere existence justified it.

Today's traveller is better equipped than those of the Renaissance, as he can study them in the nearby "Museo dell'Opera del Duomo", where the originals are now on display, safe from the dangers of the weather, together with the delightful *Cantorie* by Donatello and Luca Della Robbia from the doors of the sacristies of the Dome.

One is always sorry to see a work of art removed from its original context; but sometimes it is a cause for rejoicing, as when a fresco or a mosaic, for example, is taken down from a lofty or obscure position and made accessible to the eyes of those who might appreciate it. For that reason, photographs, whether in the form of films or art-albums, are now an essential companion of the discerning traveller.

A general view of the city from the Piazza della Signoria, with the cathedral towering over the scene.

Above, detail of the façade of Orsan-
michele. Right, the Palazzo Vecchio.

The palaces of the Commune.

Between the two squares a monumental cube links the two poles of Florence—religious and civic. Orsanmichele worked for the commune before going over to the church. The sculptures on its four faces confirm his dual loyalty, as they are the patron saints of the guilds, the famous *Arti*, which ran the destinies of the city. They were carved out of stone by the finest artists of the *Quattrocento:* Ghiberti, Donatello, Verrochio. Inside, a fourteenth-century tabernacle by Andrea Orcagna formerly housed a miraculous picture of the Virgin, which was burnt and replaced. This wildly Gothic work is out of proportion with the monument which contains it.

After the plague of 1348 it was decided to dedicate to the Virgin the loggia which acted as the base for this imposing granary. Talenti

was called in to alter the building, enclose the loggia and decorate its façades. Despite the master's skill, the utilitarian architecture of Orsanmichele lacks spiritual elevation.

A little way further on, at the edge of the Piazza della Signoria, stands the much prouder Palazzo Vecchio. The rigorous style of this building, the sheer size of its tower and its windows and battlements strongly reflect the power of the city when it was at its height. The name "old palace" is something of a misnomer: it was built to stand astride the centuries and withstand the events of history. It has not failed in its mission.

In the eighteenth century, at this very spot, some Ghibelline dwellings used to stand on the ruins of the Roman theater. They were destroyed after the victory of the Guelphs, and it was decided that the site should be used for the construction of a communal pal-

ace. It was built, under the direction of Arnolfo Di Cambio between 1299 and 1314. The Gothic military style finds a most suitable expression in the majesty of the tower, a sort of cantilevered belfry which is still truly the "lighthouse of the city", in both meanings of the term. For more than seven centuries it has witnessed the major events of the city below. In 1478, Archbishop Salviati and half a dozen conspirators in the pay of the Pazzi were hung from the windows of the Palazzo. In 1492, Savonarola came to power here. Five years later he was burnt to death, in the middle of the square where, only a year before, he had tossed books, objects of art and pictures which were, in his uncompromising view, licentious, onto the "bonfire of human vanity". During the 15th and 16th centuries the Piazza della Signoria was the preferred place to hold public festivities, tournaments and the ball game known as *Calcio,* which still takes place in the traditional costumes of the Renaissance. A plaque at the foot of the Palazzo Vecchio reminds the visitor that he is standing at the spot where, on 11 August 1944, the liberation of the city was celebrated. Today, there is no public gathering or festival in Florence which does not end in the piazza, which is gaily decked, for the occasion, with tapestries and banners bearing the city emblem—a red lily.

It is essential to visit the inside of the palace, which abounds in historical memories, and also to climb up to the path along the top. One forms an even more striking impression of the sheer size of the place by walking into the huge Grand Council hall, and seeing the monumental stairways and the elegant courtyard, which is always so cool in summer. The charming *Child with a Dolphin,* by Verrocchio, which adorns the fountain, contrasts with the majesty of the general background, as does the *Studiolo,* where Francesco de Medicis kept his treasures locked up, with the sumptuous quarters of Leo X, the second Medici pope.

Above and right, ornamental motifs from the façade of the Palazzo Vecchio.

36

REX REGVM ET
DOMINVS
DOMINANTIVM

The Palazzo Vecchio: left, the façade. Above, the chamber of the "Five Hundred", built by Simone del Pollaiolo and renovated by Vasari. Below, the inner courtyard, by Michelozzo.

Various views of the Piazza della Signoria with the Fountain of Neptune and the statue of Cosimo I de Medicis (1594).

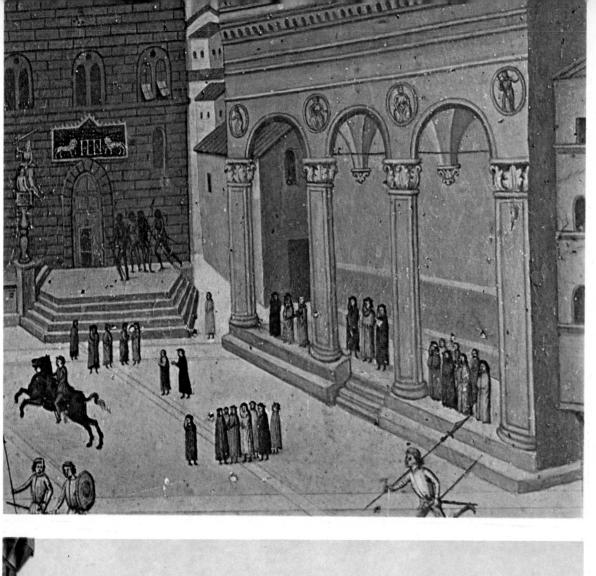

From the Signoria to the Bargello.

Like most of the squares of Florence, the Piazza della Signoria impresses one because of its diversity and lack of balance, rather than by a sense of grand order, as is the case with some squares in Rome or Paris.

Facing the Palazzo Vecchio, the elegant arcade of the Loggia dei Lanzi contains a small open-air museum. Built in 1380, it served as a guard-house for the "lanzi" of Cosimo I—whence its name. Now it is home to a number of prestigious sculptures—both originals and copies—dominated by the haughty figure of *Perseus,* by Benvenuto Cellini. Outside the entrance to the palazzo is a copy of Michelangelo's *David,* and a fountain in which my nymphs and satyrs frolic under the huge but gentle figure of a Neptune who is jokingly referred to as "il Biancone"—the "big white one". Further on, a statue of Cosimo I on horseback by Bologna, is Florence's tribute to the memory of the first Grand-Duke of Tuscany (1519-1574), who tried to restore the prestige of the city after the return to power of the Medicis.

A short distance from the Palazzo, on the Piazza San Firenze, stand two other "light-houses" of this city, the Badia belltower, and the crenellated tower of the Bargello. The Badia Fiorentina, a monastery which dates from the year 1,000, contains one of the most charming works by Filippino Lippi, the

Apparition of the Virgin to Saint Bernard. And the church itself, somehow *not* on the standard tourist circuit, offers a haven of silence in the heart of the city.

Just opposite, the Bargello—the former palace of the podestat, the foundation of which dates back to the 13th century—houses the national museum of Tuscan sculpture. One wonders whether there can be any other city on earth where the art of shapes is so prominently represented as in Florence. From Donatello to Michelangelo, from Verrocchio to Bologna, the great masters of sculpture have decorated its squares and its palaces. Their works include themes from both the Bible and mythology, legend and history: *David* by Donatello, and *Mercury* by Bologna, *Bacchus* by Michelangelo, and *Ganymede* by Cellini... All this, and terra cottas by Della Robbia, bas-reliefs, works in ivory, tapestries and jewelry go to make up a whole which is dazzlingly rich.

Here again, the horrors of history are covered over by beautiful works of art. The Bargello, which was built for the *podestat* and borrowed his name, was both a prison and the residence of the chief of police. The chapel was where Savonarola spent his last night before being burnt at the stake. The Bargello had its own chamber; until the 18th century, a scaffold, decorated with sculpted shields, used to stand in the court-yard. This stern building evokes the tragic

side of the centuries of Florentine grandeur just as effectively as the Palazzo Vecchio.

On either side of the axis—now heavily devoted to the tourist trade— which joins the Duomo to the Palazzo Vecchio, and more particularly near the Bargello itself one enters a web of narrow streets bordered by tall houses, which five one a good idea of the way Florence must have looked in the Middle Ages. The Casa Dante is a reconstruction, dating only from the beginning of the century, which was erected in the poet's honor. Yet the district is precisely the one in which he was born, while the nearby church of Santa Margherita used to be under the patronage of the Portinari, the family of Beatrice, the young Florentine girl who was the inspiration for the poems of the *Vita Nuova.* Beatrice died at the age of 24, in 1290; this adolescent love became, for Dante, the idealized image of woman, and, in his major work, the *Divine Comedy,* the symbol of Christian thought in relation to Virgil, who symbolized the culture of Antiquity.

Born in 1265, the son of Florentine nobles, Dante Alighieri fought with the Guelphs, was elected to the Council of the commune, and tried to reconcile the Black and White factions within the Guelph party. When the Whites eventually triumphed, the poet was forced into exile. He died in 1321 at Ravenna, where his ashes were buried, far from the city which he had, at various times, both

45

Dante's house, with a bust of the poet and a commemorative plaque.

MCMXI
TRA LA CHIESA DI SAN MARTINO DEL VESCOVO
E LE ABITAZIONI DEI DONATI E DEI MARDOLI
SORGEVANO CONTIGVE LE CASE
DI BELLO E BELLINCIONE ALIGHIERI
E NELL'AVITA DIMORA NACQVE DANTE

IL COMVNE DI FIRENZE
SI ASSICVRÒ IL POSSESSO DEL LVOGO
E SVLLE VESTIGIA DELLE ANTICHE CASE
COSTRVÌ QVESTO EDIFICIO
PER NVOVA PVBBLICA ONORANZA
AL DIVINO POETA

Facing, contemporary miniature showing Dante writing the Divine Comedy. *Below, plaque naming the places which the poet used to frequent.*

Hall and bedroom in the Davanzati palace.
Right, bottom, an ornate wardrobe from the
Davanzati palace.

loved and cursed.

Opposite this medieval quarter, on the other side of the Piazza della Signoria, stands an area occupied by the palaces of the great Florentine families, the Davanzati, Rucellai, Antinoni, Strozzi, which, with their massive embossed façades, have a most grandiose and stern appearance. While wandering down the streets which run along the bank of the Arno, in the midst of these palaces, the visitor will discover some interesting churches: San Apostoli, a Romanesque basilica with three naves, Santa Trinita, with a Baroque façade and frescoes by Ghirlandaio. Some distance further on, facing the river, the church of Ognissanti, founded in 1256, also has a Baroque façade dating from 1638. One of its chapels is dedicated to the Vespucci family, one of whose sons, Amerigo, was a navigator who gave his name to the continent of the New World. The tombs of Sandro Botticelli and Caroline Bonaparte are also here. Ognissanti also contains a precious relic: the cloak worn by St. Francis of Assisi at Alverna when he received the stigmata. In the adjacent cloister his story is related in fresco form; there is also a justly renowned *Last Supper* by Ghirlandaio, which is thought to have been the inspiration behind that which Da Vinci later painted for the Convent della Grazie in Milan.

The construction of the Palace of the Officies (Uffizi) *was undertaken by Vasari, on the orders of Grand Duke Cosimo I. Two views of the palace.*

The treasures of Florentine art.

It is perhaps significant that the guilds which, beginning in the Middle Ages, brought Florence its prosperity, should have been called *Arti,* the Arts. They encompassed all activities: there was the art of wool, the art of money changing, the art of clothiers and even that of the grocers! With the passage of time the meaning of the term changed, but its origin seems to suggest that, for Florence, art was more than a form of its activity, and that it was the very stuff of life for the city.

Cimabue (1240?-1302) and, more particularly his pupil Giotto (1266-1337) were men of the Middle Ages. They were the heirs of Byzantium, though they did not draw very much on this heritage. In the words of Suares, "Giotto looked at the world in which he lived; miraculously, he saw it." Giotto was a friend and contemporary of Dante; and, like him, he was a precursor of major developments, in that he drew on tradition, but in order to free himself from it. He set in motion the vast undertaking known as the Renaissance, proclaiming a new era in which man would become aware of his full nature, and in which he would open up new paths towards the future, while at the same time seeking inspiration from the sources of Antiquity, instead of renouncing the past. The chisel of Renaissance sculptors and the brush of its painters were to bring into being works in which the saints of Christianity and the gods of ancient Greece stood side by side. Marsilio Ficino, who was both philosopher and religious, tried to unite Platonic doctrine to that of Christianity. From the beginning of the 15th century—the *Quattrocento*—there was a prodigious blossoming of talent which gave Florence the greatest concentration of works of art ever assembled in such a small space!

Yet this new self-awareness never caused the artist to stand apart from his own people. These masters, whose genius has towered over the centuries, never ceased to be craftsmen, working to order, being paid for the skill they had learned... They were members of the *Arti,* and the revolution initiated by the innovators made it clear that this humility in no way contradicted their creative accomplishments; instead, it was both a condition and a consequence of them. It was because he restored man to the center of the universe that the artist of the *trecento* discovered movement, gesture, feeling, and invented perspective in order to show things not as they were, but as man saw them.

There are three names which, early in the 15th century, stand out in the three artistic disciplines: Brunelleschi (1377-1446) in architecture; Donatello (1386-1466) in sculpture; Masaccio (1401-1428) in painting. We have already met the first of these in the

Duomo, with the cupola of Santa Maria, and the second in the Bargello, with Orsanmichele. We shall find Masaccio on the other side of the Arno, in the church of Santa Maria del Carmine.

Brunelleschi worked at Santa Maria from 1420 to 1436; he also collaborated in the construction of numerous other buildings which we shall come to later. Having worked first as a goldsmith, and then as a sculptor, he left the distint imprint of his style on Florentine architecture.

Donatello began as a pupil of Ghiberti. This friend of Brunelleschi gave statues a sense of vitality and an expressive intensity which can be admired in the *Crucifix* of Santa Croce, the astonishing *David* at the Bargello, and the bas-reliefs of the lively *Cantoria* in the Opera del Duomo.

Masaccio, who died at the age of 27, perhaps poisoned, played a similar innovative role in painting. He brought to completion the work begun by Giotto and showed unprecedented liberty in his composition and color; he truly brought life back into painting.

This Florentine school of painting spanned three centuries, from Giotto to Michelangelo, and all of it is to be found within the walls of the Uffizi gallery, which runs from the Palazzo Vecchio to the quays of the Arno. It is one of the richest museums in the whole world, particularly for Italian painting.

In a work such as this we cannot possibly

list all its treasures. Instead, one should try to form a general impression of the entire school, its majors names and most characteristic works, and trace its dominant features as they appear in infinitely varied forms, contrasting in a gentle harmony with the austerity of the architecture and the rigor of the sculpture of Florence.

The buildings of the Uffizi, which provide such an exquisite frame for the view of the Palazzo Vecchio which one gets from the quay, were built on the initative of Cosimo I to accomodate the archives and offices *(ufizzi)* of the city. Naturally enough the works of art acquired by the Medicis found their way there too; and it is in this way that the present collections of the museum were built up.

As one enters, one is immediately impressed by the "Virgins in Majesty" by Cimabue and Giotto, which still bear the hieratic imprint of Byzantium. After Masaccio, here represented by a Madonna, the Renaissance makes a powerful statement with the large painting by Paolo Uccello (1397-1375) entitled the *Battle of San Romano.* The sheer sophistication of Uccello's art would meet the most modern of standards: he painted his horses red and his meadows blue, and went well beyond realism in geometrical compositions which he enriched with arabesques.

Fra Angelico (1387-1455) was without doubt the last mystic in Italian painting. Fra

53

Lippo Lippi (1406-1469) was a monk, like Fra Angelico, though he was hardly an ascetic at heart. He eloped with the nun who was posing for his *Virgins,* and she bore him a child, Filippino Lippi, who was later to become a pupil of Botticelli, himself a pupil of Filippo Lippi. Between them, these three painters brought to the images of the Virgin a juvenile freshness, more worldly than sacred, which makes them more human and more accessible to twentieth-century man. This delicacy of touch and bitter-sweet tenderness reached its highest point in the work of Sandro Botticelli (1445-1510), the most secret of all the painters of the Florentine school, and, at the same time, one of the most endearing. A brilliant selection of his work occupies a whole room at the Uffizi, pride of place going to two of the most famous ol all Italian paintings, his *Birth of Venus,* whose unique blend of languor and charm is surely unequalled, and *Spring,* a work which, despite its title, really seems to express the dual triumph of life and death; the central figure of this latter painting is the beautiful Simonetta.

A great deal has been written about the work of Botticelli and his complex, disturbed character, which eventually yielded to the mystical exaltation of Savonarola. Botticelli, painter to the Medicis, was among those who tossed into the flames works of theirs which the accursed monk had judged to be licentious. Botticelli's *Virgins* were close to Venus; he painted them with the same melancholy tenderness, thus giving a plastic expression to the precepts of Marsilio Ficino. Another trait found in Botticelli, as in so many other painters of the Florentine school, particularly Gozzoli, is a fondness for exquisitely refined oriental decorative motifs.

The beauty of the works assembled here is so overpowering that it is quite impossible to wander aimlessly through any part of the Uffizi. One *has* to go back, devoting whole days just to one section, moving on to the masters of the end of the *Cinquecento,* a period when Botticelli was sinking into a

religious crisis and preparing his own purgatory, and when two other Tuscans were approaching the height of genius. Leonardo da Vinci (1452-1519) and Michelangelo (1475-1564) are represented in the Uffizi by paintings of their youth: the former by the *Annunciation,* a work from the studio of Verrochio, who had been Leonardo's master, and the *Adoration of the Magi,* which remained incomplete. As for the latter, there is a *Holy Family* which shows the remarkable sense of relief which was to serve Michelangelo well in his work as a sculptor.

The Uffizi also contains some of Raphael's finest *Virgins.*

GIOVANNI BOCCACCIO

BENVENUTO CELLINI

GUIDO ARETINO

GALILEO GALILEI

DANTE ALLIGHIERI

FRANCESCO PETRARCA

The great men of Florence, seen in the sculptures which adorn the Uffizi Gallery.

NICCOLA PISANO

GIOTTO

MICHELANG. BUONARROTI

LEONARDO DA VINCI

DONATELLO

NICCOLÒ MACCHIAVELLI

3. SANCTUARIES OF BEAUTY

Moving outwards from the ancient Roman forum, Florentia grew to become the city of the Middle Ages and Renaissance whose narrow streets and whose churches and palaces we have just visited. From that period onwards, the further growth of the city required the construction of new districts, which grew outwards in a fan-shape on the north bank of the Arno.

The sixth set of city walls, built between 1284 and 1333, was able, with its ramparts and towers, to contain the city until the middle of the 19th century. To begin with, however, new buildings went up in the center of town, between two of the most remarkable churches of Florence, Maria Novella, in the west, and Santa Croce, in the east.

Further north, the Medicis built their palaces and the church of San Lorenzo. The churches of San Annunziata, Santa Maria Maddalena de Pazzi, the Foundling Hospital, the convent of San Marco, and the Academy of Fine Arts, all signal other stages in the aesthetic history of Florence, and are all home to numerous exquisite works of art. It is these buildings, whether sacred or secular, that we have chosen to call the sanctuaries of beauty.

From Santa Maria Novella to Santa Croce.

In this book we do not seek to "guide" the reader along a strict itinerary. Instead, we would like to point out certain relationships

Two famous Florentine churches: left, Santa Maria Novella, and, below, San Lorenzo.

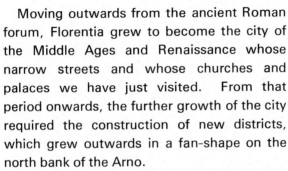

Views of the Campanile, the cloister and the interior of Santa Maria Novella.

and to propose a choice, leaving the reader free to arrange his own itinerary as his fancy or his preferences take him.

The entire old city separates these two basilicas, which almost look like boundary markers. Santa Maria Novella is the Dominican church, while Santa Croce is Franciscan. Both look out over huge squares, in which the ordinary people of Florence come and go about their daily business. The two churches seem to be attracted towards each other in some mysterious way, like the poles of the two religious orders which were to have such a profound impact on later centuries. Indeed the faith of Florence is in a sense embodied in a symbolic architectural tryptich: the Dominicans and Franciscans standing watch over the city gates, each of them the same distance from Santa Maria dei Fiori.

The visitor to Santa Maria Novella is first struck by the façade, perhaps the most elegant in the whole of Florence. There is ample space in front of it, on the square of the same name, to get a good view of its white and green marble arches, which run from the main door, both right and left, towards the former cemetery and the cloisters. It even manages to hide the tall spire of the bell-tower under a pediment and scrolls which add significantly to the charm of the whole structure. Geometrical designs abound: squares, diamonds, triangles, rectangles and curves, all as if some child had strewn them about playfully. While the façade is Romano-Gothic at the base, it has a wealth of Renaissance ornament, paid for by the Rucellai family, about the main entrance. Construction started in 1278 and remained incomplete for many years, finally being concluded in 1470 from designs by Alberti.

Inside is a tall, slender nave, with two side naves leading to the chapels of the Rucellai, Strozzi, Gaddi and other families. The visitor will note the wooden crucifix by Brunelleschi, the fresco by Masaccio, and, above all, in the chapel of the high altar, an admirable series of frescoes by Domenico Ghirlandaio, painted between 1485 and 1490. In these works, with their noble composition, poetic attitudes and wealth of coloring, Ghirlandaio is clearly seen as one of the great masters of his age. The son of a goldsmith, he was born in Florence in 1449, spent some time in Rome, where he had been summoned by Pope Sixtus IV to work on the Sixtine Chapel, after which he soon returned to his native city, where he died in 1494. He was the protégé of the Tornabuoni family.

The green cloister leads to the Spanish chapel, the walls of which are entirely covered with frescoes by Andrea di Buonaiuto (1355), blending scenes from the gospels with allegories of the Church militant and triumphant. The ambition of the motifs is not matched, however, by the harmony of the composition.

Two of the narrow winding streets which enable the modern visitor to Florence to recapture, even today, the mood and spirit of another age.

Outside the church of Santa Maria there are lawns with pools and with obelisks standing on bronze turtles. These obelisks acted as markers for the chariot races which took place from the 16th to the 19th centuries. Before that time, the crowds used to come here fore more spiritual reasons—sermons and mysteries. Today children play, pigeons fly and tourists rest their weary feet in front of this façade, whose harmonious balance and diversity of styles so nicely sums up the spirit of Florentine art.

The Piazza Santa Croce, another favorite place for a stroll, lies at the other end of the old town, just outside the Franciscan church. On its central terrace, children play football between the beautiful façades, some of which are decorated with frescoes, of the 16th-century houses.

Early in the 13th century, the small tradesmen of this quarter, which is situated outside the walls, used to come and listen to the Franciscan friars in a small church dedicated to the Holy Cross. Arnolfo di Cambio was asked to design a replacement for it in the 13th century; he turned it into the largest of all Franciscan churches. Work on it lasted more than a century, and it was not consecrated until 1443. Curiously, the façade, like that of Santa Maria dei Fiori, is nothing but a neo-Gothic overlay from the mid-19th century!

As soon as one enters, one is overawed by

the majesty and the vast sweep of the three naves. Under a ceiling of polychrome wood, on either side of rows of pointed arches, stands a king of Florentine Pantheon. Michelangelo, Ghiberti, Machiavelli and Galileo have their tombs here; most of these were done by Vasari, in emphatically allegorical form. Dante is honored by a cenotaph, while his ashes remain in Ravenna,

Like Assisi, Santa Croce has a great deal of work by Giotto on the theme of St. Francis. The frescoes in the Bardi chapel—and particularly the saint's death—are among the artist's most outstanding works. Recently, purists have covered up "those parts which were not painted by the master himself". The whole general effect to the composition has thus been marred by unsightly blotches of plaster, which were placed there for the sake of a "personal authenticity" which, in the Renaissance studios, simply did not exist!

Giotto is for Santa Croce what Ghirlandaio is for Santa Maria Novella. He displays a sense of grandeur and an economy which give him an extraordinary position in the world of painting, and not merely in that of his own period. Giotto (1266-1337) was a pupil of Cimabue. His work as a painter, in Florence, Assisi and Padua is his most striking accomplishment. At Santa Croce one also finds samples of the art of Brunelleschi in the Pazzi chapel (1428-1442), which stands next to the basilica itself, at the end of the cloister. It is a marvel of finesse and balance, and is decorated with medallions by Donatello and Luca Della Robbia.

The Florence of the Medicis.

North of the Piazza del Duomo, Via Martelli leads towards Via Cavour, formerly known as Via Larga on account of its breadth and straight layout, which contrasted sharply with the narrow streets of the medieval quarters. It was built on the orders of Cosimo the Elder, founder of the dynasty of the Medicis, who, by building his palace at the corner of this new road, caused the center of Florentine life to shift northwards.

Michelozzo began work on the palace in 1444, from a plan which was later to inspire the whole of Florentine architecture: a square structure, closed off from the outside world, with an inner courtyard decorated with sculptures, and a garden. The Medicis family lived here until 1540. During the time of Lorenzo the Magnificent, it was the setting for a brilliant court which received artists, scholars and poets. Kings and princes stayed within its walls, including Charles VII of France and Emperor Charles V.

After the decline of the Medicis the palace was sold to the Riccardi family for 287,000 pounds. They altered it a great deal, and gave it their name. Almost all that remains of the 15th-century structure is the private chapel, which is well worth seeing on account of its fresco by Benozzo Gozzoli entitled *The Procession of the Wise Men on their way to Bethlehem* (1459-1460). The story told

by this fresco unfolds like a film on the walls of the chapel. In keeping with tradition, the artist painted the characters from the gospel in the costumes and the setting of contemporary Florence. He even gave the legendary figures the faces of members of the Medicis family—in particular Lorenzo the Magnificent, in the guise of a Wise Man, riding a white horse. Gozzoli's spirited style is well exemplified by this lively fresco, which is tinged with a most fetching oriental influence.

The Riccardi palace now houses the police department, but visitors are allowed into the Luca Giordano Room, the vault of which bears an *Apotheosis of the Second Dynasty of the Medicis,* which is well suited to the Baroque exuberance of the late 17th-century gallery.

A few yards from the palace which witnessed their glory—where Giovanni, the future Pope Leo X, and Catherine, the future queen of France, spent their early years—the sacristies of San Lorenzo contain the tombs of the most illustrious members of the family. More than anywhere else, this is the Florence of the Medicis.

The church of San Lorenzo was their parish church, in the midst of a very ordinary residential district, full of that "popolo minuto" which was to provide Cosimo the Elder with the basis for his power. Before him, Giovanni de Bicci had invited Brunelleschi to rebuild the original church in a style worthy of his

Above, statue in the courtyard of the Medici palace. Right, the splendors of the Chapel of the Princes, in San Lorenzo.

own ambitions. San Lorenzo is a vast building with three naves lined by Corinthian columns and semicircular arches; it contains works by Donatello—two pulpits decorated with bronze panels—and his tomb. Brunelleschi's Sagrestia Vecchia is adorned with sculptures and reliefs which are also his work. Verrochio was responsible for some of the sarcophagi containing the ashes of several members of the family.

The visitor will note with particular interest the Sagrestia Nuova, or Chapel of the Medicis, built by Michelangelo, which houses the tombs of Giuliano, Duke of Nemours, and Lorenzo, Duke of Urbino. Michelangelo sculpted for these tombs four allegorical figures, *Day, Night, Dawn* and *Dusk,* which rank among his very finest masterpieces. Lorenzo and his brother Giuliano lie in another tomb, for which Michelangelo was able to sculpt only the *Madonna and Child,* and which is incomplete.

Other Medici tombs are in the exquisitely ornate Chapel of the Princes. The beautiful cloister next to the church leads to the Laurentian Library, also built by Michelangelo, which contains an incalculable wealth of rare manuscripts and irreplaceable works.

Portraits of Lorenzo and Giovanni de Medicis.
Right, detail from an equestrian statue of Cosimo de Medicis.

One of the great families of History.

The Medicis were originally from Mugello, a hamlet to the north of Florence, and they were certainly country people. Having settled in the town to engage in business, they soon came to occupy an enviable position. In 1314, Ardigo de Medicis was gonfalonier and was responsible for the triumph of the popular party which drove the poet Dante into exile. In 1378, Silvestro de Medicis supported the revolt of the *Ciompi,* or wool-carders; it was by means of popular support that the Medicis, after they had become bankers, and while continuing their business activities, later came to assume an ever more dominant role in the affairs of the Republic.

Giovanni de Medicis, the father of Cosimo the Elder, was treasurer to the Vatican. For thirty years, from 1434-1464, his son was to be the master of a city which he himself had helped rise to its position of pre-eminence. Though on less familiar terms with the public than his grandson Lorenzo— nicknamed, somewhat inaccurately, the Magnificent—Cosimo the Elder (1389-1464) was truly the "Father of his Country", as he used to be called. He did not seek honors for himself, choosing instead to hide his ambitions under the affable manner of a monarch. Pope Pius II once wrote to him saying "The only royal attribute that you lack is the title of King". Briefly banished by the Albizzi, who supplanted him, he went into exile in Padua, and later made his way to Venice. A year later he was recalled to Florence, where he crushed his rivals, hanging some and sending others into exile. Cosimo conducted his affairs and those of the city with equal skill; he lent money to the pope and to the king of England. He established a public library and a Platonic academy, made Marsilio Ficino his protégé, kept the confidence of his people and did much to promote ancient culture and the arts. Besides being the father of his country, he was also the father of the Renaissance.

His son, Piero the Gouty, was a puny creature who remained in power for only five years. His wife, Lucrezia Tornabuoni, from a rich Florentine family, bore him two sons, Lorenzo the Magnificent (1449-1492) and Giuliano (1453-1478), who was assassinated by the Pazzi.

Lorenzo was a complex character who had inherited from his grandfather a great political ability, while his mother gave him a poetic mind. He was a tyrant in the original sense of the term, or, as Guichardin put it, "the best and nicest tyrant imaginable". He was ruthless in crushing his enemies, such as the Pazzi conspirators. In business he was less successful than his forebears, and allowed foreign subsidiaries to founder unnecessarily. He loved banquets and festivities, organized Roman-style triumphs and, like Nero, listened

to the Muses: "Ah! the beauty of fleeting youth! He who wants to be happy should be happy, for tomorrow is uncertain". He was also a powerful patron of poets and artists. He died at the age of 44, in 1492. Two years later, a bankruptcy and the curses of Savonarola brought discredit to his family. Thus came the end of the first Medici dynasty.

The second came to power in 1512, only this time by force, with the support of Pope Leo X, one of the sons of Lorenzo the Magnificent. The government of Florence in fact became one of the States of the Church. The city of independence once more expelled the Medicis in 1527. They returned in 1530, with the help of the now-reconciled pope and emperor. Alessandro (1510-1537), Lorenzo's bastard son, first duke of Florence, was assassinated by his cousin Lorenzino. Cosimo I, son of Giovanni dei Bande Nere (1519-1574) Grand-Duke of Tuscany, made the Medicis a princely family which was later to give France two queens, Catherine, wife of Henry II, and Marie, wife of Henry IV.

Cosimo I, truly an "enlightened despot" if ever there was one, made his grand-duchy into a genuine State. Could it be that this political figure was the monster who was alleged to have poisoned two of his daughters and his father-in-law, stabbed to death one of his sons, and, as if that were not enough, committed incest?

The two monks of San Marco.

From the Medicis-Riccardi palace, Via
Cavour leads to the Piazza San Marco, which
stands on the site of the former Via Larga,
the link between the palace and an old 12th-
century monastery in which the Dominicans
established themselves in the 15th-century.
As compensation for money acquired through
business deals and money-lending Cosimo
the Elder made a grant of 10,000 florins
towards the reconstruction of the church
and the expansion of the convent of San
Marco. He placed his own palace architect,
Michelozzo, in charge of operations, and
went ahead in such style that he ended up
by paying more than 40,000 florins!

The church designed by Michelozzo was
altered by Bologna in the 15th-century in a
Baroque style. The façade is from the 18th
century. Inside are the tombs of the two
great thinkers of the period: Angelo Poliziano and Pico della Mirandola, who was
prodigiously gifted as a child.

The great painters of the Florentine school
have their privileged sanctuaries. Ghirlandaio
is at Santa-Maria-Novella, Giotto at Santa
Croce and Masaccio at the church of the
Carmine. However, the concentration of
works by a single artist is nowhere greater
than at San Marco, the artist in question
being Fra Angelico.

This monk from Fiesole was instructed by

some portraits and some reminders of that strange meteoric episode in the city's history. the prior to paint frescoes on the walls of the friars' cells. For Fra Angelico painting was in itself a sort of prayer. Aided by some pupils, he painted his visions of heavenly glories, from the Annunciation to the Transfiguration. His Christs were laden with symbolism. Fra Angelico, the most mystical of the Florentine painters, was, however, a painter before he became a monk. He made the break with the world in 1407, when he was about 20, and dedicated his painting to God. Yet he considered his painting to be divinely inspired, and for that reason refused to make subsequent alterations, saying: "If my work has come out this way, it is because God so willed it."

He lived at Orvieto, Florence and Rome, where he died and where he was buried. But he is present here, not just in his frescoes, but also in the paintings of his that have been assembled at San Marco... They have a fresh candor about them, a gentle harmony. In 1455, Fra Angelico took his place in paradise.

... Florence is a city of contrasts: less than forty years later, another monk, originally from Ferrare, was appointed prior at San Marco. His name was Girolamo Savonarola. He had a scrawny face, a blazing stare and a vehement way of speaking. He cast an anathema over the joyous city where Lorenzo the Magnificent reigned supreme. The mobs, already cowed by his gloom-laden predictions, fearfully awaited the end of their long-cherished independence at the hands of foreign invaders. He openly condemned the anti-Christ who ruled over Florence.

But Lorenzo and Savonarola were not to be reconciled, despite the formers wishes. One Lorenzo the Magnificent had disappeared from the scene, and his son had opened the city gates to the French under Charles VIII, chaos and rebellion ensued. Savonarola came to power, reformed the constitution, restored a democratic government, but took his fanaticism to the point of building a "bonfire of vanity", onto which he wished to throw all secular images.

Having been excommunicated for rebellion against the pope, he was arrested, hanged and burned.

Past the doors of the monks' cells at San Marco, at the end of a long corridor, lies the cell once occupied by Savanarola. It contains

About the Annunziata.

Some 200 yards from the Piazza San Marco there is another square, SS. Annunziata, bordered on three sides by elegant porticoes which make it one of the most charming spots in Florence. The oldest of these buildings is the "Ospedale degli Innocenti"—or Foundling Hospital—the portico of which was designed by Brunelleschi and decorated by Andrea Della Robbia (1463) with terra cotta medallions depicting babies in swaddling clothes.

The church, which occupies another side of the square, was originally a modest sanctuary of the Serviles, dedicated to the Virgin Mary. It was rebuilt in the middle of the 15th century by Michelozzo; the Atrium which was added about that time contains frescoes of the 15th and 16th centuries. The highly ornate Baroque interior contrasts with the austere looks of the other churches of Florence. The contemporary nave actually disappears beneath the decorative work added in the 17th and 18th centuries. Chapels and funeral monuments—including those of some of the Medicis and of Andrea del Sarto—were erected within. The "Cloister of the dead", next to the church, contains other tombs, particularly that of Benvenuto Cellini.

The third portico is that of the Confraternity of the "Servi di Maria" for which the church was originally built.

The Piazza San Annunciata.

We are reminded yet again of the Medicis in the Casino Mediceo, on the Via Cavour, where Grand-Duke Francis I used to keep his studios, and in the "Chiostro dello Scalzo", which has some frescoes by Andrea del Sarto—though of course it is possible to argue that one is reminded of Florence's most famous virtually at every turn throughout the city. Further on, at the corner of the Via San Gallo, the 14th-century monastery of Santa Apollonia contains the principal frescoes painted by Andrea del Castagno on the story of Christ. This artist was discovered by the Medicis in his village of Monte Falterona, whence they took him to Florence and put him to work, particularly painting portraits of famous men and women. These portraits, which, being painted against a rather neutral background, create a remarkable impression of relief, may also be seen in the monastery.

While in this part of town, the visitor, particularly one interest in the stones of history, will certainly want to visit the Archeological Museum: its collections range from Egyptian art to Roman antiquity, and are especially rich in Etruscan sculpture, painting, vases and jewelry discovered in Tuscany, the former Etruria.

Nearer the University, still very much alive with students and decorated with the graffiti of dissent, is the Galerie dell'Accademia, with its superb collection of the works of Michelangelo. The large figures sketched out by

77

Facing, bust of Michelangelo.

the artist for the tomb of Jules II seem to be straining to break out of the amorphous marble; they give one a unique impression of creative force in action. In a rotonda the visitor will see the culmination of that creativity: the original of the prodigious *David,* copies of which can be seen on the piazzale Michelangelo and the Piazza della Signoria. This statue was commissioned by the Republic in order to mark its fidelity to the principles of freedom.

Several interesting paintings by Toddes Gaddi, including the *Stories of Christ and Saint Francis of Assisi,* occupy some nearby rooms.

Three geniuses of the Renaissance.

Michelangelo Buonarotti, who had been born at Caprese in 1475, was only thirteen when he was admitted to the studio of Ghirlandaio, with whom he worked for one year. Then he joined the students who were studying sculpture in the gardens of San Marco. Having attracted the attention of Lorenzo the Magnificent, he was received at the palace, where he made his first sculptures. About that time Michelangelo was in touch with the great thinkers whom Lorenzo had invited to his court: Marsilio Ficino, Pico della Mirandola and Angelo Poliziano. The death of Lorenzo and collapse of the power

Facing, portrait of Pico della Mirandola. Below, the house of Michelangelo.

The house in which Leonardo da Vinci was born, with ornamental details of the window and the plaque at the entrance.

of the Medicis greatly upset the young artist. He fled to Bologna, and did not return to Florence until the Republic had been proclaimed by Savonarola. His career was to alternate between his home city and the pontifical court, where Julian II invited him to design his tomb and to paint frescoes in the Sixtine Chapel. Michelangelo was a sculptor, even in his paintings; his greatness is already visible in his *Holy Family* in the Uffizi, and in the cartoons of the *Battle of Cascina* which was to adorn the Grand Council Chamber of the Palazzo Vecchio.

Leonardo was 23 years older than Michelangelo. He was born in Vinci, a village near Florence, and at the age of 17 entered the studio of Verrochio, who soon recognized his superior merits. At 30 he left Florence for Milan, where he became the military engineer of Cesar Borgia. He returned to Florence in the early 16th-century, but did not stay there; like Michelangelo, later his rival, he left the City of the Flowers as its decline began to make itself evident.

Leonardo da Vinci, the most universal of the geniuses of the Renaissance, was as much a scientist as he was an artist. In the words of Elie Faure, he was "the only man in whom science and art merge as media for the expression of thought."

In 1504, while Michelangelo and Vinci were busily engaged in the battles of the Palasso Vecchio, Raphael Stanzio arrived in Florence, having already built up a great reputation with his work in Umbria for the Perugini. He was 21 years old. His later work was deeply influenced by Vinci. However, like his seniors, he too was called to Rome by the pope, and it was in this latter city that his talent reached its fruition. For these three exceptional artists the City of the Flowers was a valuable source of two centuries of tradition and creativity;

The famous Ponte Vecchio.

4. A BALCONY OVERLOOKING THE ARNO

In the 2nd century a bridge was built over the Arno, directly along the axis of the street leading to the south gate of Florentia. A new district soon sprang up on the left bank of the river; its name was, and still is, the Oltrarno. It developed mainly within the flat triangle of land stretching to the west. The Oltrarno extends as far as the hills to the south, from Monte alli Croce to Monte Uliveto, each of which is only a few hundred feet high. Yet their altitude is sufficient to provide the balcony from which we earlier dreamed of gazing out over Florence.

The Oltrarno is a working-class district inhabited by craftsmen working in hundreds of small-scale enterprises, in the areas surrounding the major squares of San Spirito and Carmine. Beyond the stern lines of the Palazzo Pitti, the Boboli Gardens, the façade of San Miniato and the Belvedere fort, the orchards and cypresses which grow at the very gates of the city form a prelude to the Tuscan landscape of the hinterland.

First, however, one has to cross the river by the Ponte-Vecchio, which is a kind of clasp joining the two banks, Fiorenzia and the Oltrarno.

Evenings on the Ponte-Vecchio

The title "Old Bridge" is well merited. It is the oldest bridge of the entire city, and the only one left standing by the retreating Germans in 1944.

The present structure dates from the 14th century, but the bridge had existed ever since Roman times. As early as the Middle Ages it already had a lengthy history: on Easter Sunday, 1215, a young noble by the name of Buondelmonte was murdered for his failure to marry the daughter of the Amidei, as he agreed to do by contract. On the appointed day, the young lady's family waited in vain for the bridegroom at the end of the bridge. To avenge this affront, the assassination of the perjurer was carried out by arrangement at the same spot. Of course, this kind of thing was commonplace at the time—were it not for the fact that this particular instance set in motion the centuries-long battle between Guelphs and Ghibellines!

The disastrous floods of 1333 swept away the original bridge. It was replaced by a more solid structure which also happened to accomodate a host of butchers' shops, it being most convenient for their owners to toss their scraps over the side into the Arno!

It occurred to Cosimo I that such a foul-smelling trade ill befitted this bridge, so he reserved it for goldsmiths and jewellers, who are still there today. Behind this double row of shops, overhanging the river like something straight out of a fairy-story, are the living quarters of the merchants. In the middle of the bridge is a loggia, with a bust of Benve-

Various views of the Ponte Vecchio.

Bridges of Florence: during the Renaissance and in modern times. Right, dusk over the Arno.

nuto Cellini, which offers an enchanting view of the two banks of the Arno and the neighboring bridges.

More particularly in spring, when the sun sets along the axis of the river, the subtle and fine Tuscan sky takes on the most delicate hue.

When evening comes the shop windows are barricaded up with tough iron or wooden shutters, after which, at least for the past few years, the Ponte-Vecchio becomes the preserve of the fly-by-night jewellers... In the middle of the bridge, which is fortunately reserved for pedestrians, young men and women clad in "hippie" clothes, spread out their wares on the ground: artfully carved costume jewelry, belts and other leather objects... Illumination is provided, at least in part, by candles or small lamps. The tourists, who find it great fun, flock along as if they were attending a party. The sellers of these goods are from Florence, Rome, Athens or Saigon, while the buyers are from Paris, London or New York... Much talking and haggling takes place. A girl wearing jeans, her legs dangling over the river, watches the dusk fade into night, while, at the foot of the parapet, two or three musicians strum away at their guitars or play the flute...

Cars are permitted on the Lungarni, yet one no longer seems to hear them. Evenings on the Ponte-Vecchio bring out the full charm of the city, and enable the passers-by to indulge in their finest daydreams...

Just after the war people used to sit on the rubble at the end of the Ponte-Vecchio. The new houses built there manage not to spoil the general style of the site. The other bridges were blown up, even the Trinita, the next one downstream; Ammanati had built it between 1566 and 1569, with two pillars and three arches, in a nice combination of daring and grace. Plays used to be performed here, apparently, and it is also thought to be the spot where Dante first met Beatrice. It was rebuilt in 1957, most faithfully, and is once again adorned with statues of the seasons. Beneath, the capricious Arno flows on, occasionally, as in November 1966, causing disastrous floods.

The district of San Spirito

At the southern end of the Ponte-Vecchio is a lively intersection which forms the entrance to the Oltrarno. In order to discover the various aspects of the city's south side the visitor will have to take each of the roads which radiate from this point in turn. Right opposite, the Via Guicciardini leads to the Palazzo Pitti; to the right, the Borgo San Jacopo leads to San Spirito, while on the left some rather steep gradients lead up to the Belvedere and San Miniato.

To begin with, we shall take the second of

these roads, the Borgo San Jacopo; the houses on the right back onto the Arno, while, on the left, one looks down a succession of charming narrow streets, with occasional glimpses of beautiful gardens situated behind the customary tall and gaunt façades. The Piazza San Spirito is very close. Its center is occupied by a garden with a fountain and statue, but it also contains the neighborhood market, as well as the church of the same name. Brunelleschi was the architect, while the work was carried out by Manetti. A bell-tower was added in the 16th century, but the façade was not finished. San Spirito is a basilica with three naves, and a total of 36 grey stone columns. It houses works of art of various periods. The former monastery next door is now home to the Romano Foundation, which has a large number of fine sculptures.

Though originally a working-class district, this veritable web of narrow streets was greatly enriched in the 16th century by the palaces which the courtiers of the grand-

name. Sometimes it is said to have a bad duchy in the Palazzo Pitti built for themselves here. The curiosity of the tourist will certainly be excited by this amazing mixture of year on the chapel, then left for Rome, where he died in 1428, at the age of 27, without fulfilling his immense potential.

Yet the frescoes which he did leave, particularly those of the story of Saint Peter, make this young artist the precursor of the Pictorial Renaissance. One century after Giotto, who never really broke away from the medieval hieratic style, Masaccio painted things exactly as he saw them, in a less stern and less monumental style. He steered painting towards the naturalism which was to pervade it for the next five centuries. His faithful rendering of expression, his flexibility of posture and accuracy of perspective were also new at the time. Like Donatello in sculpture, Masaccio brought life to art. One has only to look at *Adam and Eve expelled from paradise,* crying out their grief, to realize that, with Masaccio, painting had truly entered into the spirit of humanism.

Sixty years later, Filippino Lippi finished some of these frescoes. Yet the path had already been traced out—a fact for which we are indebted to Masaccio.

Beyond the Piazza del Carmine, in the same picturesque area, stands the Borgo San Frediano, with the church of the same ancient and often shabby houses and the splendors of princely dwellings. As he strolls

through this area his eye will alight on a gateway bearing a noble's coat-of-arms, or a wrought-bronze knocker on a sculpted door, or perhaps a Baroque fountain in the courtyard of a palace.

San Spirito is where the craftsmen have traditionally lived and worked; their workshops and stalls can still be seen there today. This is one tradition which, being an important part of the Florentine economy, was fiercely defended by its practitioners as the banality of mass-production began to make itself more and more evident.

Santa Maria del Carmine is the other pole of the Oltrarno. Here, as at the Annunziata, devotion to the Virgin Mary was responsible for the original church built by the Carmelites in the 13th century. In 1771 it was destroyed by fire; only the façade—now stripped of all ornaments—and some of the chapels in the transept escaped the disaster. The central nave was rebuilt; the Brancacci chapel, a gift of a rich 15th-century silk merchant, was luckily preserved. The frescoes which it contains make this chapel a landmark in the history of painting: they were the work of Masaccio, a young pupil of Masolino. At the time, he was 25; he worked for one

reputation! By the Lungarno Soderini and Ponte della Vittoria one can link the right bank to the Piazzale Vittorio-Emmanuele, a major intersection leading to the Cascine. This is a complex of gardens, with a race-track, sports-grounds, tennis courts, and promenades along which, 24 hours a day, Florentine ladies of a certain type stroll up and down, wearing miniskirts and leather boots...

The treasures of the Palazzo Pitti

We shall now return to the Ponte-Vecchio before tackling the slopes of l'Oltrarno. Beyond the Piazzetta S. Felicita, with its oft-remodelled church, the Via Guicciardini leads to the Palazzo Pitti. No.16 on the same street is the house where Machiavelli lived and died, and; further on, opposite the palace, is the house where Dostoievski stayed. The palace towers, fortress-like, over the piazza.

It was begun in 1458 from plans drawn up by Brunelleschi, for Luca Pitti, a rich banker who, ten years later, was involved in a plot against the son of Cosimo the Elder, Piero the Gouty, and lost his palace as a result. Cosimo I, the first grand-duke of Tuscany, set up court there.

The palace was enlarged, and two wings added, in the 17th and 18th centuries. Under the reigh of Giovanni-Gaston de Medicis (1671-1737) by all accounts, it became a genuine brothel. Anne-Marie Louise (1667-1743), the last of the Medicis, bequeathed the family collections to the Tuscan State.

And it is they that now constitute the wealth of the Palazzo Pitti, even more than

its elegant chambers and gardens. The Palatine Gallery contains 500 paintings, mainly from the 16th century, and not only from the Florentine school, but also from the Romanesque, Venetian, Spanish and Flemish schools. Works by Raphael, Andrea del Sarto, Titian, Tintoretto, Velazquez and Rubens are the pride of this gallery.

The Museo degli Argenti has ten rooms full of magnificent objects either received as gifts by the Medicis or ordered specially by them, including vases, goblets, cameos, embroidery, porcelain, etc. The sumptuous royal apartments are a most suitable setting for such treasures.

The Palazzo Pitti stands on the lower slopes of the hill. To the rear, it extends thourgh the Boboli Gardens, which were started in 1549 by Trebolo, on the orders of Cosimo I. Laid out in the Italian manner, these gardens are grouped around a central promenade decorated with statues, and comprise a number of coppices, caves and fountains—the whole effect being a nice blend of the rigor of man's intelligence and the fancies of nature.

The Boboli Gardens stretch westwards as far as the Romana Gate, and eastwards as far the Belvedere Fort, the terraces of which provide some excellent views of Florence.

In order to get there, however, one has to return to the Ponte-Vecchio and make one's way up the Via della Costa di San Giorgio, where Galileo's house, No. 14, can be seen. The Via di Belvedere, flanked by old walls and olive groves, takes one to the Piazzale Michelangelo.

The Boboli Gardens and the Pitti Palace.

The hill of San Miniato

The Ponte San Niccolo and the Viale dei Colli are the commonest routes, at least for the motorist, to the Piazzale Michelangelo. The avenue climbs in a series of broad curves across the wooded slopes of the hill. The Piazzale Michelangelo, now dominated by souvenir shops and tourist coaches, is a broad platform on which a group of castings of the artist's main Florentine works was erected in 1875.

From the terrace the entire city can be seen, complete with domes, towers and the beautiful ochre tint of its rooftops. Down below lie the Arno and its bridges, and the plain, which runs from Florence to Pistoia... Beyond the receding contours of the hills one can see the Apennine peaks standing out against the bluish haze of a sunny day. To the rear there is a 16th-century loggia, now in service as a coffee shop, and the tiny church of San Salvatore al Monte, which Michelangelo used to refer to affectionately as his "lovely little peasant girl". The remains of the fortress built by Michelangelo before the siege of 1530 can be reached by paths deep amongst the pines and cypresses.

From the terrace of San Miniato, which is bordered with railings and cypresses, the view is more restricted, though perhaps even better, on account of the beauty of the environment. San Miniato al Monte has a splendid façade of white and green Prato marble; it was built in the 13th century, but the origins of the church go back to the 3rd century, and to the death of the martyr Minias, who is buried under the cypresses. The first structure was rebuilt in about 1018 in the Romanesque style. The lower part of the façade dates from that period, and the building, seen as whole, is the most harmonious exemple of Florentine architecture.

In the middle, a mosaic of Byzantine inspiration—Christ surrounded by the Madonna and Saint Miniato—flashes with golden reflections at sunset. The eagle of the Arte di Calamala, the guild which renovated the church, soars over the pinnacle of the building.

Inside, we find the same harmony: three naves separated by rows of arches decorated with geometrical motifs, Renaissance chapels with terra cotta work and sculptures, and a ceiling of polychrome wood. The choir is divided into two levels, with the high altar and the monks' choir in the upper part, and the Romanesque crypt below, its vaulted ceiling supported by a multitude of columns which make the crypt look rather like a mosque. Its starkness contrasts with the wealth of decorative detail in the nave and choir. The tombs and the relics of the martyred saint lie at the end of the crypt.

Near San Miniato, the Bishops' palace, restored in the 19th century, looks out at the world through beautiful twin windows.

Left, overall view of the hill of San Miniato.
Facing, the church of San Miniato, and, below, detail from the pediment of the church.

On the wat down, the visitor may wish to follow the Via dei Colli, as far the Via San Leonardo, a small, quiet road which winds along past old mansions and heavily-wooded estates. Tchaikovski lived in one of these houses, marked by a plaque; it is remarkable for its balconies, which one immediately notices from the road. Eventually, the Via San Leonardo leads to the Belvedere.

On the left of the photograph shown above, the Belvedere.

Facing, a house once inhabited by Tchaikovski, who was one of several foreign artists who came to live in Florence.Right, Via San Leonardo.

96

The monastery of Vallombrosa.

5. VILLAS AND MONASTERIES

The beauty of Florence also lies in its countryside. The hills on either side of the valley of the Arno make up a harmoniously balanced landscape in which the presence of man—villages and bell-towers—blends discreetly into a green setting. One would almost say that the silvery green of the olive-groves had been designed specially as a contrast to the dark green of the cypresses. Vines form garland shapes between the trees; roads which must surely date from Antiquity wind their way across the fields from one hamlet to another.

Westwards, and downstream, one has the full impact of the 20th century: railroads, suburbs, factories. Instead one should turn south, in the general direction of Pian dei Giullari, where one will find the charming churches of Santa Margherita a Montici and San Michele a Ripaldi. But first of all, one should turn northwards, towards Florence's mother city, Fiesole, which provides the finest views of Florence and the surrounding region.

The Etrusco-Roman city of Fiesole

The origins of Fiesole certainly go back to the 6th century BC, though it is first mentioned in the history books in connection with the defeat, in 285, of the Etruscans by the Roman legions. Fiesole then became Faesulae, the Roman, but it was destroyed in 80 BC, when it sided with Marius against Sylla.

The ruins which lie spread out along the hillsides of the Mugnone valley date from this period. All that remains of the Etruscan period is a gate and a few sections of wall. It is in the Florentine city that the traveller alights, whether from automobile or coach, onto a vast and lively square bordered with "ristorante" and "trattorie" to suit all tastes and all pockets.

This square, named Mino da Fiesole in tribute to the sculptor who worked for the Medicis, is also bordered by the bishop's palace and the dome, with a crenellated bell-tower which looks out over the old city.

The original building, from 1028, has been enlarged and embellished. It has a simple exterior; the interior contains works by Mino da Fiesole. The ruins of the Roman theater, discovered in 1809, are nonetheless the major attraction of Fiesole because of both their archeological value and their superb location. The theater, which was improved by Claudius and Septimius Severus, is in the form of a semi-circle, with a sweeping view which encompasses the Mugnone valley as far the Mugello hills, in the area where the Medici family originated. Here, as in the Arno valley, on the other side of Fiesole hill, the landscape is a joyous contrast between olive-groves and cypresses. The ruins consist of the thermal baths and an Etrusco-Roman

The hill of Fiesole.

temple. Sculptures, vases, funeral urns and other Etrusco-Roman objects have been assembled in a small museum at the entrance to the ruins.

The left part is adjacent to the hillock on which the convent of San Francesco stands, at some 1,000 feet above sea level. In front of it there is a terrace which offers a view of Florence and the Arno valley as far as the distant Apennine peaks. Visitors will certainly relish the blissful calm of the inner cloister. The convent also contains the cell once inhabited by Saint Bernardino of Sienna.

From the terrace of San Francesco and the Piazza Mino da Fiesole the old road provides a pleasant walk down to the village of San Domenico da Fiesole, about half-way down. On the way one walks past the estates of several famous villas, the most famous of which is that of the Medicis. This simple country house was built by Michelozzo for Cosimo the Elder, who used often to receive classical scholars there, among them Ficino.

The 15th-century church has a fresco by Fra Angelico. Nearby, is the Badia Fiesolana, a former cathedral which still has its 11th-century Romanesque façade. Brunelleschi most fortunately respected it when he rebuilt the church in the 15th century.

At the foot of Fiesole hill is the Villa Palmieri, which is strongly reminiscent of the Decamerone. It was the setting for a number of stories told by a group of young men and women who had taken refuge there during the plague.

Such villas—the luxurious "secondary residences" of the notables of Florence during its golden age—are to be found throughout the vicinity of Florence. They, too, are rich in souvenirs and form an elegant and graceful contrast to the stern visage of the same families' townhouses. Rulers and bankers used to come out here, into the Florentine countryside, to forget their cares. However, many of these villas are still privately owned estates and are thus rarely open to visitors.

An early palace and Roman columns at Fiesole.

The Florentine villas

Under the aegis of the Autonomous Tourism Agency of Florence a "Committee for visit to the gardens of the finest Florentine villas" has been formed. It is the only organ authorized to arrange visits, which take place in motor-coaches, from April 1 to June 30. Each weekday afternoon, the programme includes visits to three gardens, chosen from among a dozen or so residences. And, even though these visits are confined to the outside of the villas and their gardens, they are still very much worthwhile. Since they take the visitor out to the high ground surrounding Florence they also provide an opportunity to take a closer look at nearby sites of interest.

While most of these villas are Renaissance in appearance, and were often remodelled subsequently, some of them date back to earlier periods. For example, the Villa della Petraia, a former castle with its tower and sentry's patrol path, which, in the 14th century, was the scene of some bloody fighting between Florentines and Pisans. At the end of the century, the castle was transformed by Buontalenti for Ferdinand de Medicis into a princely villa, with a garden and a grove of holm-oaks and cypresses. This building which enjoys a superb situation overlooking the plain of Florence, was remodelled in the 19th century, and became the preferred residence of Victor-Emmanuel II, while Florence was the capital of Italy.

The Villa del Castello, near the Petraia, was bought in 1477 by the Medicis, and

*Left, the villa where Milton once lived.
Facing, a typical Tuscan landscape.*

embellished by Lorenzo the Magnificent. Beyond a chestnut-fringed drive it can be seen with its curious centrally-located dungeon, and a terraced garden by Tribolo (1540) which has fountains, grottoes and statues. Now it is State property, and, when completely restored, is to become a musuem.

Another venerable residence, the Villa "I Collazi", was built by Buondelmonti in the second half of the 16th century, presumably from Michelangelo's plans. Its white façade stands out on a hill; it is surrounded by cypresses and has a spacious terrace which offers a magnificent view of the Chianti-growing slopes.

Another villas whose gardens are open to tourists is the Villa Peruzzi, which has an Italianate garden with a pond. The dungeon seems straights out of an ancient castle. The Villa Rondini belonged to the Brothers of the Holy Trinity, and then to a famous 19th-century actor; it is now a hotel.

It is also possible to see the gardens, pool and chapel of the Villa Capponi and those of "Il Giullarino", which have been so lovingly kept up by their owner. The same is true of Villa la Pietra, belonging to a British historian, Sir Harold Acton, which is wooded with a splendidly harmonious blend of pine, cypress and boxwood. Assorted statues and cupids decorate the verdant theater and the temple, with all the grace of the 18th century.

Lastly a word about Villa Arrighetti, which has often been remodelled since the 15th century and Villa I Tatti, bought in 1905 by the famous art critic Bernard Berenson. It was here that he wrote the greater part of his works. When he died in 1959 Harvard University inherited the villa and his collections and set up an institute for the study of Mediterranean art and culture.

Other Medicean villas

Many other villas—including some very impressive ones—are not listed by the Committee on Tourism. Among these is the most famous of all, Villa Carreggi, where Cosimo the Elder used to receive the humanists, and in particular Marsilio Ficino (1433-1499), who was in a sense his spiritual son, and at the same time his master of philosophy. Cosimo once wrote to Marsilio Ficino: "Only yesterday I arrived at my Villa Carreggi, moved less by a desire to improve my land than to improve myself. Come and see me, Marsilio, as soon as you can, and do not forget to bring with you the book by your divine Plato on the sovereign good. I shall spare no effort to discover true happiness. Come, and remember to bring with you the lyre of Orpheus."

Marsilio Ficino was the canon of San Lorenzo. In the words of the historian Funck-Brentano, he was a "frail, puny man, a melan-

The Medici villas at Pietraia
and Poggio a Caiano.

choly, gentle dreamer, who commented on the works of Plato while trying to establish links between them and the gospel... Ficino became the center of the philosophical movement in Florence under the Medicis. His renown extended as far as France, Germany, England and Hungary. He knew the leading figures of his age, kings and princes, prelates and men of letters."

Marsilio Ficino was thus the basis for a sort of bond between the wisdom of the ancients and Christian doctrine. Pope Pius II said: "Christianity is nothing more than a new, more complete reading of the sovereign good of the ancients." Not long afterwards, Raphael painted, on the walls of the Vatican, *The Triumph of the Holy Sacrament* and *The School of Athens.*

Cosimo the Elder died at Carreggi. His descendants, Piero the Gouty and Lorenzo the Magnificent remained faithful to the traditions of the villa. Lorenzo used to assemble gatherings of scholars, scientists and artists. Angelo Poliziano (1454-1494), tutor to Lorenzo's children, poet and philosopher, wrote in Greek, Latin and Tuscan. At the age of twenty, Pico della Mirandola (1463-1494), a thinker with prodigious powers of memory, was already the *protégé* of Lorenzo. In 1468 he was condemned by the Roman Curia, fled to France, was imprisoned for several weeks at Vincennes, and eventually returned to Florence. He died

young, poisoned by his secretary. He was only 31. At 23, in his *Discourse on the dignity of man,* he ascribed the following expression of his ideas to God, who was addressing mankind: "We have not made you either celestial or terrestrial, or mortal, or immortal, so that you, as a free, sovereign modeller and sculptor of yourself, might be able to sculpt yourself in whatever form you choose. You might degenerate and fall towards the lower level of beings, the animal world; or, it you wish, you may regenerate yourself and rise towards the superior beings who are divine."

Carreggi was the scene of the secret meeting between Savonarola and Lorenzo de Medicis, who was then on his death-bed. Marcel Brion has described the end of the Magnificent One, at the age of 43, in his superb villa: "Poliziano and Pico della Mirandola stood at his bedside, silent. The poet and the philosopher contemplated the battle between man and destruction; they could offer him no comfort or consolation. Lorenzo was about to die; outside the windows, the Florentine spring radiated all its sweet glory."

Poggio a Caiano, above the spring named l'Ombrone, celebrated by Lorenzo and his friends, was another villa close to the heart of the Medicis; it has an ancient peristyle, a vaulted ceiling adorned with an incomplete fresco by Filippino Lippi, a long terrace, with railing, overlooking the gardens...

102

Abbeys and monasteries

Besides the Medicis, the monks wielded a notable cultural influence in the Florentine countryside. One of the finest religious entities of the region is the monastery of Galuzzo, founded in 1342 by Nicolas Acciaciuoli, a Florentine friend of Petrarch and Boccaccio, and high constable of the kingdom of Naples, where he had made his fortune. The large ensemble of buildings stands at the top of a hill covered with olive-groves and cypresses. Construction lasted over several centuries; the first occupants were the Carthusians of Saint Bruno. The church has a 17th-century façade and a rood-screen. There are Gothic stalls, Baroque decorative work, tombstones of the Acciaiuoli family in the underground chapels, and, most notably, a large open-air cloister, with a marble well and 77 medallions by Giovanni Della Robbia. The Cistercian monks manufacture herbal medicines and liqueurs.

Galuzzo is on the road to Chianti. Even before one reaches the monastery, one passes yet another Medici villa, this time Poggio Imperiale, which has been occupied since 1864 by a girl's school. Beyond the monastery lies the village of l'Impruneta, which is the scene, in mid-October, of a famous fair in honor of Saint Luke.

Some eight miles west of Florence is the abbey of San Salvatore a Settimo, a 10th-century structure remodelled in the 15th. The interior has three naves, with frescoes and enamelled terra cottas.

It is possible to make a very fine excursion, by car or public bus, to the monastery of Vallombrosa, founded in the 11th century by Saint Giovanni Gualberto, who protested against the usury of his contemporaries. The monastery played an essential role in the reform of the church; indeed, from 1035 to 1065, it was the center of a spiritual renewal in Florence. Nowadays it houses a school of forestry. The road leading to it climbs up the Val d'Arno, through Tuscan landscapes which have a distinctly Alpine appearance. The buildings—and a hotel and restaurant—are situated in the midst of a pine forest. Slightly higher up, at 3,300 feet, is a solitary house known as Paridisino, where Milton once lived. Further on, towards Arezzo, stands the highly impressive Franciscan monastery of Alserna.

Left, two views of the monastery of Galluzo. Facing,
a farm in the Chianti-growing area. Below, a typical
landscape from this region.

On the Piazza della Signoria…

6. THE SEASONS AND THE DAYS

Which is the best season for a visit to Florence? This region, which is open to the northwest, and closed towards the southeast by the barrier of the Apennines, generally has the same climate as northern Italy. Winter is cold, and spring often comes late. Summer can be very hot indeed; so that the best time of year to enjoy the charms of the Florentine part of Tuscany is spring—May and June—and autumn, which means September and October.

One should not forget that the beauty of Florence lies also in its sky and its light, since it is these qualities which explain why the painters of the Florentine school made their rural backgrounds so gentle, and the faces of their models so tender.

The moderate warmth of its bright sunny days is conducive to a casual stroll. The vegetation of Tuscany keeps its principal adornment of olive-groves and cypresses both in springtime, with its new spirit of hope, and in the nostalgia of autumn. Even in winter, this landscape, on certain fine days, can show its full beauty to the visitor.

It is important to *stay* in Florence, rather than just pass through on a visit. The sheer abundance of impressive monuments, and the phenomenal wealth contained in churches and museums alike tend to push the tourist close to saturation point, beyond which he is no longer able to enjoy the pleasures of the city. A casual approach to the City of the Flowers is by far the best. One should be prepared to be indulgent towards aspects of modern life, such as the platoons of tourists converging on Duomo or Palazzo, which tend to spoil the magic of the place. But one should always accord the same degree of attention to this city, which has never lost its former identity.

In the words of André Suarès, "Florence is a sacred place, which positively breathes intelligence." Anatole France spoke of the "ethereal quality of the Florentine light which caresses beautiful shapes and inspires noble thoughts." This passage occurs in a novel which is now almost forgotten, a tribute to the city entitled *The Red Lily*—this being the emblem of Florence.

The people of Florence.

Between the Duomo and the Palazzo Vecchio, the Piazza della Repubblica is a square, in the proper sense of the word, surrounded by gaunt buildings which are so ordinary-looking that the guide-books say nothing at all about them; this is a square which is for the people of Florence much more than for the tourists. But it is relaxing. Some open-air cafés stretch all the way into the middle of the square. Here the tourist can rest without having to endure much motor traffic, since it has been banned, as at many other points of heavy tourist concentration, except for taxis and buses. Incidentally, this is a wise measure which the tourists might well try to implant in their own countries!

Piazza della Repubblica is a thoroughfare and a meeting-place for busy people; originally it was the site of the Roman forum, where municipal affairs were debated; and today it is still the setting for many a discussion of business or politics, under the arcades. There could be no better spot, therefore, to look at the men and women of Florence, said to be the most elegant in Italy, as they go by. André Suarès, in his *Journey of the Condottiere,* has this to say: "A handsome people, lively and sophisticated, with slightly dark complexion, sparkling eyes, and crisp, sharp gestures: all them are well and neatly dressed, their shoes shiny, their felt hats soft and clean. They have a singing, if somewhat hoarse, accent: it is well rounded, fluid, gay and caustic at the same time, and there is nothing flabby about it."

Children's faces and women's faces suddenly stand out in the crowd, because they are so like the models for a fresco by Ghirlandaio or a relief by Donatello. And the women? As Suarès puts it, "they have astute features, and a capacity for laughter, yet with few outbursts, a curious blend of boldness and timidity... The gift of mockery, and a slight edge of sarcasm which implies a distrust of sentimentality..."

But are foreigners good judges of such things? Yes, judging by the observations of a Tuscan from Prato, Curzio Malaparte: "There is something whimsical about Florentines, perhaps their brazen, bantering air, a unique capacity for mixing laughter with speech—in a word, an elegance, a spirited fantasy which makes them the most pleasant, the most unusual and the most dangerous of all the peoples of Italy." And the author of *Kaputt* also wonders "what is the charge most commonly levelled against us by foreigners—that we are too intelligent or too free?"

This selfsame freedom and intelligence are traits of the history of Tuscany, and, accordingly, of the Tuscan character. "It cannot be by pure chance that the Tuscans have always been a free people, in fact the only one in the whole of Italy which has not tolerated foreign oppression and has always governed itself..."

Malaparte, in his delightful essay in self-criticism—quite as bantering and gay as the Florentines themselves—entitled *Those damned Tuscans,* adds: "We have always chosen our tyrants from among members of our own family: the home-bred variety of tyrant, you might say."

Right, the symbol of a gentle life-style.

Fun and festivities.

Only privileged persons on a long stay in Florence could say, like the French writer Montesquieu in the 18th century: "We go into houses where they have silver lamps on the table, and, all about, plenty of pretty, gay and witty women..."

It is much easier—and quite as fascinating—to see the way the ordinary people live, and, above all, the way they go about their daily business, in the small shops which sprout up, during the season, under the loggia of the New Market. Cheap souvenirs, handmade curios, prints and scarves occupy this rectangle, next to the flowers, fruits, vegetables, and, of course, those red water-melons which Florentines so love.

The loggia of the Mercato Nuovo was built in the 16th century. The visitor simply *must not* fail to stroke the snout of the bronze *Porcellino,* by Pietro Tacca, which stands guard near the market.

Apart from the wealth of sights and smells one experiences on a trip to this market, it is also a source of information. There are others, also, some of them even less touristy than this one, particularly the San Lorenzo

market, which also happens to be close to the central market. Flowers are to be found at every turn in the city of the red lily...

While the city's housewives are to be seen in the market, one has to go to cafés to hear male Florentines, of all classes. The Piazza della Repubblica is not the only place where they have open-air cafés, which are such a pleasant feature of this country. There are others—even nicer—in the Piazza della Si-gnoria, where, just like in olden times, horse-drawn cabs await or deposit their customers. On that square, opposite the dignified pa-lazzo, the terrace of *Chez Rivoire* is *the* place to go for the best chocolate!

Like Rome or Paris, Florence has its literary coffee-houses; for example, the *Michel-angelo,* on via Cavour, and the *Giubbe Rosse,* once a favorite haunt of Unamuno, Gide, Papini, together with Montale, Vittorini

and other opponents of Fascism.

Throughout the city one finds an abundance of *ristorante, trattorie,* and *pizzerie.* The local cuisine has some special delights: "Bistecca alla fiorentina" is known beyond the boundaries of Tuscany, but there are also "fagioli all'olio" (beans with oil), "crostini" (bread slices with poultry livers and herbs) and "papa al pomodoro" (bread broth with garlic and tomato sauce), all washed down with Chianti, which is grown in abundance in this region. Moreover, in a myriad little bars one can nibble, at any time of the day, on "salami" and "panini tartufati", or bread rolls stuffed with white truffles and eaten with marsala or white wine.

The musical and theatrical festival known as "May in Florence" has an international reputation. Also, in May and June, there is the traditional ball game played in period costumes, the "Calcio", which we have spoken of earlier. There is also the feast of Saint Giovanni, patron-saint of Florence, and that of the Virgin Mary, in September; on Ascension Day there is the curious festival of the crickets, in Cascine Park.

A foudness for festivities led Florence to play a prime role in the birth of opera. From the 15th century onwards, the Carnaval accompanied its mascarades with ballets. In 1540 the *pastorale* was created. In 1590 *Aminta,* by Torquato Tasso, was played to music in Florence. About the same time,

Count Bardi del Vernio assembled a group of musicians—the "Camerata"— which invented the representative style which later led to the birth of opera. Peri, Rinuccini, Cavalieri, in charge of the minor entertainments at the Tuscan court, had pastorales played. On the occasion of the marriage of Maria de Medicis to Henry IV, Rinuccini and Peri wrote *Euridice.*

Every event of any note at all was a pretext for processions and lavish displays. For the second marriage of Francesco de Medicis to Bianca Cappelli, the merrymaking lasted ten days. Even funerals were couched in theatrical form. Vasari took twenty pages to describe that of Michelangelo, on July 14 1564, with a catafalque 50 feet high, adorned with painted statues.

200 years later Grand-Duke François-Etienne of Lorraine abandoned Florence to settle with his wife Maria-Theresa, heiress to the imperial throne, in Vienna. Henceforth, Florence took its leave of its masters, who, as Malaparte would have put it, were in any case "no longer home-bred".

The age of the Medicis, with its splendor and its drama, has passed never to return. Florence had turned the last page in the most exciting chapter of its history.

Left-hand page, a market and night-time festivities on the Piazza della Signoria. Following pages, the cathedral and the Campanile of San Miniato.